a body, in spite

Alain Jugnon

a body, in spite

a slight philosophy for actors

translated by Nathanaël

Nightboat Books
New York

Atrox: that which cannot be eaten
An occasional series of works published by Nightboat Books

Copyright © 2010 by NOUS
English Translation Copyright © 2017 by Nathanaël
Published originally as *À corps défendant* in 2010 by éditions NOUS
All rights reserved
Printed in the United States of America

ISBN: 978-1-937658-75-5

Design and typesetting by Kit Schluter

Cover & Frontispiece: *Chronos lion dévorant l'enfant terre* (after Cranach
the Elder's *The Werewolf*) by Musial Jean-marc, ink on paper, 2013.
Courtesy of the artist.

Cataloging-in-publication data is available
from the Library of Congress

Distributed by University Press of New England
One Court Square
Lebanon, NH 03766
www.upne.com

Nightboat Books
New York
www.nightboat.org

Contents

A Note on the Translation

à corps défendant forces the translator's hand. If the
work, in its French, employs an unassuming syntax,
the internal relations of the sentences, some of
which are slight adjustments to existing idiomatic
expressions, results in a reader risking twisting her
neck. And since a translator is in no position, ever,
to claim immunity, the result, for the English that
follows in the wake of the French, is one of, shall we
say: consequence. If one were to resort to analogy,
one might be tempted to contend that if Jugnon's
text keeps its parts hidden on the verge of being
exposed, the translation arrives with its skirts up. It
is the same body, under different exposure, one that
could be qualified as *inverted,* since the hidden parts
of the French sentences in order to have a chance
at a life in this English stubbornly adverse to the

particular game of mirrors the French language can indulge in, without seeming silly. English has a great aversion to play of this kind, though it abounds, of course, in plenty of other kinds of play. Its internal method is direct, and its lexicon is far too articulated for the kinds of semiotic sleights of hand present here. What I mean is that French, with a much more reduced vocabulary than English, has a very dense polysemy as a result.

Take as an example, aphorism n° 51: "Jésus n'est pas mort en croix, il est mort hanté." The sentence, direct in appearances, expresses the following, literally: "Jesus did not die on the cross, he died haunted." Listening more closely, one hears the phonetic repetition of the [ã] of "en croix" and "hanté." And upon closer scrutiny still, "hanté" reveals itself as the homonym of "in the shape of the letter t"—"en t." All of which then renders moot the now heavy-footed "he died haunted." After having discarded several unfruitful attempts at reproducing the repetition internal to the French sentence, with wonderfully obsolete words such as "hontous" or "onerable," a small shift in emphasis allowed the sentence to pivot on the preposition, arriving at: "Jesus didn't die on the cross, he died to a tee," with an ambivalence now infused in the expression "to a tee." There is some question (for me) as to the relevance of this kind of explication. But in this instance, perhaps, two or three further examples are indicated, to underscore the degree to which this translation has lost its pants.

Aphorism n° 160 declares: "Mieux vaut vivre dans le faux que suivre très tôt l'homme à la faux." One needs very little encouragement to lose one's head. Literally, the sentence reads: "Better to live in falsehood than to follow early on the man with the scythe." The sentence turns on the word "faux," meaning both false/hood and scythe, and referring of course to the Grim Reaper, while rhyming the words "faux," "tôt" and "faux." English simply won't. My proposal, somewhat less ostentatious, puts forward: "Better to live and lie than to swallow the vial," in which, through several torques, "better to live and lie" is a somewhat tormented amalgam of "live and let live" in its redress under Ian Fleming's pen (the second James Bond novel, 1954) as "live and let die" as well as "let sleeping dogs lie." The "vial," which suggests, homonymally, the "vile," contends Socrates, as well, for me, as Malraux's vial of cyanide, such as were distributed to the members of the Résistance during WWII. Malraux, in this instance, is entirely of my invention. But is not out of keeping with the text whose historical markers—1940, 1987, 2007, etc.—are altogether of this lineage, and political indignation.

At n° 291, there is something of a small riot: "Pleurer une déconvenue alors qu'elles viennent de partir." Literally: "Mourn an inconvenience when they [feminine] have just left." The grammar is incoherent, with a singular referent for a plural pronoun. Eventually, the play reveals itself, and the word "déconvenue," when taken apart, sounds like "des cons venus": "some idiots [who have] arrived." There is still a lack of "proper" agreement here since "cons," an everyday word in French for idiot, which actually means cunt (French abounds in these), is, oddly enough, a masculine noun, and the phrase is declined in the feminine. The sentence itself is a fine example of revolt against convention, semantic and otherwise. My English is, alas, somewhat less flamboyant in its reach, with its preference for a similar internal rule: "Rue a misconstruction when they have shaken it down." The play here is on architecture—"rue" is a street in French, a "misconstruction" is also a misconstrual, and a shake-down is Noir's heavy hand. What the translation loses here in audacity, it gains in other (private) parts of the text.

Finally, the text's signal at n° 49 is perhaps a suitable by-word for the work of translation, generally speaking, and certainly in this specific instance: "Au commencement dire la table et ne pas savoir qu'elle est d'écoute." Literally: "In the beginning speak the table and know not that it is listening." A "table d'écoute," the expression upon which this sentence is split, is a wire tap. Behind the wiretap is, in my reading, the surveillant apparatus of monotheism with its tablets of the law, here most emphatically in its Christian (Catholic) declension. To arrive at an English that would account at least for one layer of this threat, with sufficient legibility, my proposed sentence abandons the table in favour of the wire: "In the beginning strip the wire and know not that it is tapped." One hears the trip in the strip, but in any case, the references have by this point been flung quite far afoot.

It may be a *professional deformation* as French says with such ease, to see in the wire tap, a strong signal to translation as to its permanent compromise. The translator has been called by many names, but she can never be accused of having told the whole truth.

—N.

a body, in spite

a slight philosophy for actors

Man is not the vanquisher of chimeras. He is not the novelty of tomorrow. He is imbecilic, the depository of falsehood, but he is able to understand that he is the sister of the angel.

ISIDORE DUCASSE

1. In the end, I lie down.

2. The world fits actors like a red velvet glove.

3. Remiss is the right word if one remits the slip.

4. God has his place atop the church, next to the chimney, so as not to catch cold.

5. Out of despair, man takes woman and squeezes her.

6. As a child, he lost in the exchange when the father became enamored of the mother. It's a story of names that ring more or less true in a child's ears, at the age of attunement to his future.

7. Feeling the imminence of departure and never again parting ways.

8. In the beginning saying dada and not knowing that mummers too.

9. An actor evolves on stage, sensibly and by definition, he doesn't know how to walk, or kick it.

10. God is dead like wood.

11. At the end of the run, the actor hides his costume under his skin.

12. I left the mother at birth; I knew the father in survivance; I found the child in the mirror, I died a man all evening long.

13. It is a slight philosophy for the use of actors who will usure themselves only if it profits by them.

14. Listen to the pillows, coupled to what is said, and learn everything about those two, a father, a mother.

15. The actor alone knows that there are others besides, and not the least of which, at the ticket office, every evening.

16. You cannot imagine the number of actors who live and work for the performance.

17. I speak by chance and it falls upon me.

18. What does an actor see in another actor? He sees what he hadn't bet on and what was played and lost by the latter.

19. It seems like the dawn of a new world: actors are beginning to resemble us.

20. He is clearly getting into the habit: what did he look like before the in-vestment?

21. Giving in to onanism, he loses his business sense, give or take.

22. I mean life side by side with chance and words.

23. An image is accused of having shown a hidden thing, it is inside all the heads, and the whole world ended up on its side: just an image and the world finds itself there.

24. During a terrifying first migraine, he clearly posed the problem of his life: he was born a Prussian squire, he dies an Italian highlander, and he made a clean sweep of his country and a smokestack.

25. May be: what it is may already be.

26. To each in his own domain and plug your nose when entering.

27. The actor enrolls and deserts a life.

28. To be afraid of the actor, is to dream of the man behind the heat of the mask.

29. I am nothing like a man, that is my alibi.

30. To the disorder of verse without feet, he prefers that of the fingers of a hand.

31. Since the first one, all the books I have read speak only of me; it has reached such a point that I wonder about those I haven't read; must I worry about what they have to say about me? and if these books say nothing, how can I read them, I, who am everything?

32. Believe in a truth and drink the lye of one's reality.

33. If god were chanced upon, his divinital prints would be taken.

34. Slowly darken one's thinking in order to accommodate its scope and be large before the world.

35. At the outset, without throwing the die, reaching the goal, and being at loose ends.

36. As a child, he was born without anyone noticing. The mother, questioned, speaks of a forgetfulness that night. The father, dead, doesn't remember forgetting anything. It was the wind passing through.

37. I even saw actors hold their breath, because they lived among men, so as not to have to perform.

38. He dealt the actors without shuffling them before the performance.

39. I took my fall for flight and taking stock, I decide on a total and near dispersal of my activities.

40. On the desire of men: it will be said that clouds and hats are there to hide the dirty pictures chalked onto the skulls of men.

41. To that old question, I have already found an answer, a moment ago.

42. As a child, he speaks and writes at a chance: he has things to tell it.

43. God is khâkhâ, believe in my heavy experience of it.

44. Looking straight ahead for a familiar detour and finding oneself before the third door to the right in the hallway.

45. I carry loftily in me the idea that man is base and I see clearly in me his heights and his depths, all of it, on the ground floor.

46. In 1987, the world broke its sword.

47. By chance he hears what spares him.

48. The world, which is round, turns squarely wrong: seek out and level the angles.

49. In the beginning strip the wire and know not that it is tapped.

50. On that day, I decided to leave things as they are: words will experience the rest.

51. Jesus didn't die on the cross, he died to a tee.

52. On the road, always look back and comb oneself in the mirror before leaving.

53. How does he manage to hide the long hallways that his eyes leave lit at night?

54. The sea draws her cards along the ochre beaches: it will be said that I was the first grain of sand to be touched by foggy knowledge.

55. To undo oneself of all that was done without touching the knots.

56. The real enchants me like all short stories.

57. Truth is the only lie that runs in the skirts of reality.

58. In 1987, a man, a false beard, a doll's name, irritated an upside country that prickled him and a Trial was made for a close shave that caused the ladies of France to lose their feathers.

59. Well seen, well said and already so young.

60. The truth owes it to herself to do nothing about it: otherwise what would they say?

61. My eyes are better, well it is too soon to take them out together on the paths of my mountain.

62. To know the depths, grow talons, and fly over the mountains.

63. To have the brutal knowledge of what knowledge means to say and shut it up.

64. I take away this cloud for the miseries of the world to rain.

65. As a child, he is already a man who lives alone by the force of things. He doesn't watch over the altruistic expenses, nor the benefits. He cashes out at the weekend. He knows the calculations of petty men.

66. Gloaming, the image trembles and its retransmission is interrupted: not knowing what it is up against, the image prefers to be disrupted rather than to clash.

67. Outside of chance, no necessity in the world.

68. The memory that serves actors finds itself worn when it reaches men who then are living only by first acts.

69. An actor plays his role and loses it at the end game.

70. The conductor, facing the orchestra and the music, evolves like an actor, he doesn't know how to play and the music passes over his shoulders.

71. The black doors close the noble souls of children: the golden keys are in the dressers of the fathers, the mothers; the birds strike with their beaks against the marble steps of the family homes; it will be said that this is a game and that I am a child; now, the door is closed and the papas and the mamas are holding their breath; the marble is dry, the house cold, I decide to begin a life as a bird.

72. Thinking himself one and not being one, the actor gains in each case having learned both roles.

73. Just a word to gain a step toward the improbable meaning of a mixture of noises, sounds and music; life is an opera.

74. If the pleasure-seeker makes of vice a virtue and the ascetic a necessity of chance, then I am virtuous by chance and necessitous by vice.

75. Seeing a mile away, I had time to make the rounds of myself.

76. If truth is a woman, then man is in the wrong, then woman is a lie because I am man. But if truth is a man, it's woman who is wrong, yet I am man and am always right.

77. Things are known about an actor whereas he knows nothing about us.

78. Has the impossible success of human societies that survive outside of the most limpid regions of air ever really been considered?

79. It is of public notoriety that nothing.

80. Knowing whereof one speaks and who is one.

81. It must be said that for the real man any truth is good for speaking provided it has a firm grip on the wagons of the train of stories told since childhood.

82. It will be said that you end your philosophy for today, you put on your clodhoppers, you walk in a German city, you splurge on a whore, and when you come back, your philosophy is finished off, alone.

83. A profession is a spine in the back of life.

84. Liking myself stricken, I loved her struck; liking himself stricken, he loved her striking; his adored Carmen.

85. Actors are given credit: for their roles while drawing on the accounts of their years.

86. It won't be said that an actor acts against his will, it will be recognized that he is doing something for the community of humans.

87. He had death wishes for the song of operas that were longings for airs and words.

88. Every evening, at the same hour, in a same place, an actor lodges a bullet in his head.

89. Is it a science then to seize the human soul in all of its breadth or would yet the soul in man be refuted? Could the existence of the soul be denied, upon seeing man place his two hands upon the sex at the priest's appeal?

90. In theatres, at night, men fear the gestures heavy with meaning of the actors on stage.

91. One's apparent hope is for the event of a lifetime and one is such a parent, who knows, that it will come passing through.

92. To make like an actor and take the receipts for oneself, even when the account isn't adverse.

93. How is it that an execution is more dismaying than a murder, if not because of the absence of reprisals?

94. Of women, man alone knows only one thing: what is said.

95. To be what one is due, let us first pay out of what one is.

96. Carmen: the merciless card practised death until it followed, hand in hand, on the path that leads to the harbor.

97 It was always known and yet, all life long, it will only ever be a matter of that.

98. Admire in man what signifies that the outskirts are fragile when therein lies the rub.

99. I toss the die on the theatre of operations and I harvest the insults of the armed comedians.

100. Very early, I learned to free myself of the obligation to know how to free myself, just to do as I was told.

101. What actors and actresses do together is not of the theatre's purview.

102. One has no idea and one wants the world at one's feet.

103. On the breach: the cries of children tip the scales where it hurts.

104. Think what one will of the divine and lie there all night long.

105. I have too good a sense of its deep desire to prefer to let myself be carried by the small waves of its surface.

106. God knows the music and he has forgotten to set it on his son's paraboles.

107. May he who has never erred cast his first written sentence in my face.

108. One sees the bullshit of one's similars upon hearing the laughter of those who differ.

109. One must not underestimate the force of the real during the lie-detection sessions that are religious confessions.

110. Each time that in the world an actor performs a child dies.

111. To break sugar on one's own back and have only a salacious thought for family histories.

112. What's at stake is the innocence of children as much as the stroke of luck: it comes down to loaded dice whatever their number inasmuch as one knows how to tell stories once the winning face is visible on the bedsheet.

113. Follow the way to the kitchen, cross the Matter, and don't forget the cooking time and the pepper.

114. Can a sentence written with true words lie?

115. Upon reflection, one country's view of another country only depends upon the angle described by the window and the mirror placed on either side of the border: no mention will be made of the fact that the customs officers are picked by a blind jury and never cross over to the other side of the mirror.

116. Offering to defend the cause and dying because of it.

117. Standing there, solitary and frozen, before the open door of the refrigerator.

118. If god had listened to Carmen, he would have made a whole meal out of god's little green apples.

119. Can one really claim to know all man is capable of when nothing is known of his family?

120. An actor never believes what he is told because he is constantly feeding his lines.

121. Lying down in the corner of a field, I saw the horror of a cow immaculated with its own shit.

122. When he isn't performing, the actor makes it seem like a memory lapse.

123. To take a word at the foot of its letter and raise it all the way up to the sentence.

124. To rot a relationship and keep sitting on it when it is cut.

125. To take to one heel and leave the other one in the stirrup.

126. I thought for once I had undone certain ties that bind me to death: but I mistook the strings and lost my parachute.

127. Answer to an image and, in fact, no longer swear by it.

128. —You become what you are. —How do you know it? —I was it before you. —What did you become? —What you will be.

129. Much is expected of an actor at the end of a race: his last skin, our own steps in his stride and when he crosses the line, the hope of donning his burial costume.

130. When no one is looking at them, do images look at themselves?

131. Some people will go so far as to pay to watch actors perform.

132. Of man, man only knows one thing: what he tells himself.

133. Rarely will one be mistaken if one brings virtuous actions back to diarrhaea, criminal actions back to ethylism and her dog back to my neighbour.

134. To know a thing well that one appreciates and, hiding nothing from dada, admit that it's mama.

135. Paul imposed Pierre upon his friends and put his all into it.

136. Man imagined everything: a god, a morality, a pleasure and in all he only loved two things: killing and breeding up a storm.

137. I loved without loving being without being there with you but without them.

138. The world escapes around us, because from inside we know enough to have it locked up.

139. He gets used to nothing, he lives, that's it.

140. Circularly permutate war and peace and lose sight of which one you began with.

141. God folds the devil's luck into his being the way the simpleton slips bills into his folds.

142. This one is frankly tempting his fate and being convincing loses all hope of seduction.

143. I know the end of the piece but fell on my head and have no idea what the beginning of the music is about.

144. Ring the necks of forgers, carve into the streams of pities and win the contest hands down.

145. Grasp what it takes: it means placing several blows between oneself and the world, those are the ones I'm talking about.

146. This actor has played all the roles and lacks only one title to his repertoire: myself, actor.

147. Say no more of a child and make him confess.

148. Of things a blind person only knows what he has been told; we, who have learned everything of things, might we be deaf? or mute? or what.

149. He spent the ore of his life speculating on the river courses of his small territory: was he sure he knew on what side the spring expressed itself?

150. I have no idea and therefore I don't think about it.

151. The actor seldom makes the rounds of the theatre as he is too busy inhabiting its center.

152. Actors are never inside, they are out front: it is truly a tragedy for an actor to perform face forward when it is simply a matter of covering his ass.

153. We have always wondered about it for as long as we can remember; we never remember what about.

154. As the men march past, he questions each face: what is the answer?

155. Noticing the mirror behind him, he let the seats trade then fold.

156. Hearing oneself say that one is going to say it and saying it on one's way.

157. In the study of a play, the actor reviews the owner: one has never seen the color of a curtain nor the pattern of a tapestry influence the choice of a role.

158. With a single move, he made a novel of his thoughts and with a word, he fabricated a philosophy of his stories.

159. Just as one makes one's bed, one bunks.

160. Better to live and lie than to swallow the vial.

161. When initializing his life, he made the screen erase even the first letter of his patronym: everything is yet to be done and the program is endless.

162. Are we sure we are able to see in nature that which is outside human purview?

163. This street speaks through this window and has no inkling as to the ears of this room next door, and it isn't the walls that are listening.

164. Cowards are written and do not resemble one another.

165. To undo oneself slowly of a prejudice and to be on the waiting list for the next one.

166. The secret folds of the human soul are unimpressed by the the iron boots successively kicking the ass of life.

167. Draw the life of a child and rub out the uncertain strokes.

168. Knowing death, we would be no wiser to it.

169. Are humans really seen to love one another when winter only freezes the half of them?

170. Hopefulness is what is hidden at the bottom of the safe when all the crap has flown out through the armored door.

171. I am already beginning to understand the reason for all of this, a sort of long-term special effect.

172. They don't know what they are doing, and doing nothing about it, they won't know any more for it.

173. He said, travelling around his room, opening doors and windows, to no one in particular, that, these past days, the mountain and the sea spoke to him in Italian.

174. Take children, you never know, they are sometimes bigger for it.

175. Speak ill of an actor, and doing so, steal his best role.

176. Succeed a tranquil joy pacifically and hear the trumpets without success.

177. Wholeheartedly break the Christian and break oneself in whole and in heart for a Christian woman.

178. Death, I have no idea, I know nothing about it, I hear talk of it, again, once more.

179. It was never said that god was good other than that he had the good taste not to let himself be tasted once and for all.

180. In 2007, old and ugly things were said, they were believed and certain brown and odorous friendships were lost, and so we gathered around its name alone, France.

181. The indigestible thought that occupies my mind travelled at length along my intestine.

182. One is none other at all inasmuch as another one is, a tall mother tells me.

183. You look through the bedroom window and it comes within range of the kitchen.

184. Being in the middle of the kitchen, reading the recipe in a loud and intelligible voice and breaking the Christian ideal.

185. Observe a minute the silence.

186. There is nothing one can do for an idea that doesn't know how to swim, one can only drown it in the sorrow of its detractors.

187. What can one expect of one's share if not that it is bigger than the others'?

188. He educates the child the way he drives the car whose rearview mirrors are turned toward what's coming.

189. A child said to a man that he was small.

190. God is good like a girl.

191. To dominate the true world and hang oneself among the reddening stars of communism.

192. A word is a world, short of spelling.

193. Let others say what they sense and plug one's nose.

194. While turning my gaze away from his abyss, I met with my own.

195. Discovering little by little the reason that brings forth: they are the things men and women take, I mean shots.

196. Well being how well we are.

197. The last actors are the first humans or will be nothing.

198. God places his finger on the knot while man wears his soles walking in the desert: the latter doesn't see the size of the laces that hold him.

199. To love one's neighbor without knowing how to conjugate in the future tense "conjugate in the present."

200. Actors always rely on what they are doing, the whole lie.

201. Feel the velocity of a possible breakthrough and be like a twat at the opening of the orifice.

202. Let us corroborate the actions of men, into collaboration.

203. An image persists and imagines itself to be a sign.

204. God loves Mary's children and he takes full advantage.

205. You look at the real back of the cave, you see real things stir, you understand the real reason for all in all, you go out without your key.

206. I am, when I think about it, at the origin of these words, just as the river is, when it thinks about it, at the origin of its source.

207. On the table the successive alignments order the world around the plate and allow the grains of rice not to stick despite the tears of dethroned gods.

208. God and all of his saints were the best that has been done in terms of backing.

209. In 2002, much hope was placed in 2007.

210. The actor holds to himself the secret of a humanity that is mistress of the mask.

211. Look inside the house and be hit in the face with its root contents, the warm fat of one's stomach.

212. Renounce the joy of existence, please oneself with insistence.

213. The memoirs of an actor are not of the past if not of a present always rehearsed and in the limelight.

214. Not long ago, he knew another version of the story: after the usual, came a brother, a sister, her angel, a cousin, another cousin, uncles, aunts, sometimes one still young and always a creature, another kind.

215. The actor loses a sense of realities by gaining on the essence of humans.

216. Knowing without having to ask and forgetting: woman retains, man detains, the child strains.

217. Take the conjugal bed, you see the pillows, no one hears it out but one listens; you look at the two inside, you count for them and you see it; you don't understand, you listen, with the pillows, you already know, right.

218. Slamming the door, hard, very hard, and flying off the handle, one evening, in summer.

219. Give in to anomaly, lead into a malady.

220. One imagines the dream of the other whereas the image returns a blind eye.

221. Look at that which in man can tear along the dotted line of his cowardice.

222. Allowing the world to exist all around and seeing oneself framed with the window full of the open sky at the back of the painting.

223. Say what one says and lie; don't say what one says and don't lie; say a thing, don't lie and say it; say something else, don't lie and don't say it; without lying, don't say what one says; without lying, say what one doesn't say; without lying, say that one lies and lie without lying.

224. Fall lifeless and rise up dead downright; having seen the beyond and forgotten oneself there or been bored, in keeping with one's political opinions.

225. I forget myself nastily every day that god makes.

226. Actors hear one another out so as not to be deaf to the noise of men.

227. What will love-children be told, when naturally they will tender their asses to the concupiscence of other love-children?

228. He gives jam to pigs like good intentions to greedy priests.

229. I very much enjoyed being with you, even if I had nothing to do with it.

230. Wonder why and no longer know when it was.

231. Go there with one's ears pricked and have them boxed.

232. Let's risk our thoughts on that land of thares.

233. I quite enjoyed watching you do, even if I did such that it was you were watching me, you.

234. Fate is a good divider.

235. Be it said in passing and so be it: *amor fati.*

236. Break the envelope of things and lose the address by return post.

237. The actor's voices are interpretable.

238. To the actress's ardors will the actor's vices be preferred.

239. Tell him nothing that he doesn't already know, he is convinced of the contrary.

240. That said, I am lying.

241. He tortures his soul to elude divinity whereas the latter is in black leather and has already settled the consultation.

242. The disorders of our actors bring smiles to the orderlies of our soldiers at arms.

243. Refute one's use for souls of ill repute.

244. To take a woman and lose the rest.

245. It will be said that to seek the contact of lovers all over is more sleek than to have the tact not to say what one covets in fact.

246. Behind the name of every actor is not always hidden the name of the latter's parents.

247. Cruelty to animals in children and Italians is something understandable: or else it is not to understand anything at all of the innocence of the latter.

248. I saw on this day Italian houses, tall and red; what I say of them is only good for my having seen them; sometimes something was written that I did not read.

249. It is said that everything is done sooner or later, one day or another, and you think of the clock that deploys the hours and the days in a rosary around your neck, knot upon knot.

250. I have given myself as a task to isolate from the concept what could be novel.

251. Tell lies and be in the true, reality is watching.

252. His views are truncated since he takes after the elephant.

253. Chip in to the incomparable and loser takes all, a done comparison.

254. To gain access to the real childhoods of little ones, he records the mamas and the papas.

255. Men were seen hitting their heads against sound barriers because they were deaf.

256. In 1987, the sexes of women, open and sometimes penetrated by the sexes of men, were the hot topics of right-wing rulers of France.

257. Say more or less that men are small and that, little by little, women are big: will one go without the other? prophesies the tailor.

258. You take the immutable order of the things of the viable world, you squeeze, you squeeze, it's dirty in the palm.

259. Being on form when jumping out of bed and losing the war by putting the wrong foot down: a start to the day that comes to a bad end.

260. Actors are no less men for it; women are more than that.

261. Tell all, describe everything, explain everything to the actor and see what comes of it on the stage of the theatre.

262. During his last distant voyage, he became aware of his birth home and, trying one key after another, found himself locked out; a man was passing by who, if he had been his father, would have let him in; when a woman told him he should go home, he well

knew that he had no mother; next time, he would call ahead.

263. A sophist, I write that I am it; a sage, so I think to be; a philosopher you be who read that I am so.

264. Whence the sense that life has meaning? From behind the faggot-flame.

265. Agreed with a capital A and having surrendered with a capital S, having said so with a capital S and not making the move.

266. He invents his own remedies and with internal baths purifies himself of all the indigestible matter that life has him swallow.

267. It is said that death takes upon itself all the ills commited against men: they think nothing less with regard to life and the whole bitchery.

268. To lose a bit of what one is while gaining the good graces of the magnificence of the godless sky.

269. In the corner of a field, I saw the horror of a cow endlessly chasing away flies, with its tail, its ears.

270. The round eyes see all the way down, the square head hits the subsoil, he rested his head against the bodies of women, his eyes collided against the abodes of souls, it nonetheless resembles a philosophy, a slight philosophy that one carries along.

271. Take the inroad of 40, the French were walking on the road just the same.

272. On the last day, he will surprise the world by speaking of his cow, his dog and his daughers, and it will be his son who will sit on the lid of his tomb, to continue to keep quiet.

273. One despairs truly whatever one says from the day on which one hopes whatever one does for a slight despair of convenience.

274. What is a string of chance if not the immense luck of having had the good fortune of knowing it?

275. A man takes an umbrella and gives himself a blow to the head with it: here is one manner against depression, a blow against the patter of rain, in the place of a slicker and beneath the misery of the world: look no father.

276. To hope, is to despair in reverse.

277. One never knows and yet there is nothing that isn't spoken about.

278. Make the child and burn the sketch.

279. Erase the last image then count on the next one to remember the one from before and so on.

280. In the course of a printed sentence, a word exiled itself and refuted the whole book.

281. This kind of story has been seen too much and too well understood: a father, a mother, a child, a house and at times a man, a woman, too old, that kind.

282. He's an actor, he doesn't know how to put on an act.

283. To see far and lose the detail of the coupling of beings and chains, naked.

284. God loves everything I do and wherever I do it.

285. In the beginning, say YES and learn one's name.

286. To understand one's destiny, leave it to destiny and sit on one's heels.

287. I know that I know nothing but I can very well see that it's all there.

288. To catch oneself saying, while pissing, that one can't see one's little wee-wee and to be alone.

289. Mad as he was, he lived one hundred years ago now; when he was alive, he often thought of dying; he died in 1900, at the end of his life; to no end, mad as he was.

290. When he entered the school of life, he pulled through with a dead weight in his soul.

291. Rue a misconstruction when they have shaken it down.

292. State the meeting place and lose the very idea of when it was, including the price.

293. Child, the day he learned the whole story, decided never to grow up; the many gestures Child undertook and repeated enabled him to maintain the distance; advancing one step at a time, day after day, he didn't grow by a single centimeter; the nature of his malady was such that Child remained what he was since last year, a child.

294. To read the life of the philosopher and to live to the letter thinking that is alive; to read the writings of the philosopher and to write a life that thinks.

295. Every actor will one day in his life have the opportunity to be saved by his costume and his hat: still will he have to choose them in his own size so as not to save an other than himself.

296. The actor is a centaur, half true, half false, and with angel's wings on his head.

297. This actor discovers the open and his emotions while putting on airs along its spectacular coasts.

298. In future, the true men will be real men, and truth, who is a woman, will be sad.

299. Tell the truth and get over it.

300. To live against when life is for and reciprocally, thank god.

301. I lie down, it's finished, curtain.

à corps défendant

une légère philosophie à l'usage des acteurs

L'homme n'est pas le vainqueur des chimères. Il n'est pas la nouveauté de demain. Il est imbécile, c'est le dépositaire du faux, mais il parvient à comprendre qu'il est la sœur de l'ange.

ISIDORE DUCASSE

1. A la fin, je me couche.

2. Le monde va aux acteurs comme un gant de velours rouge.

3. La paresse est le mot juste si on va par deux.

4. Dieu a sa place en haut de l'église, à côté de la cheminée, pour ne pas prendre froid.

5. De désespoir, l'homme prend la femme et s'en sert.

6. Enfant, il perdit, au change quand le père s'éprit de la mère. C'est une histoire de noms qui sonnent plus ou moins bien dans les oreilles de l'enfant, à l'époque á l'écoute de son avenir.

7. Se sentir dans l'imminence d'un départ et ne plus jamais en départir.

8. Au commencement dire papa et ne pas savoir que maman aussi.

9. Un acteur évolue sur la scène, sensiblement et par définition, il ne sait pas marcher, ou crever.

10. Dieu est mort comme le point.

11. Au terme des représentations, l'acteur cache son costume sous la peau.

12. J'ai quitté la mère à la naissance; j'ai connu le père en survivance; j'ai trouvé l'enfant dans le miroir, je suis mort en homme tout un soir.

13. C'est une légère philosophie à l'usage des acteurs qui ne s'useront que si elle se sert d'eux.

14. Ecouter les oreillers, entendre ce qui s'y dit, et apprendre tout sur ces deux-là, un père, une mère.

15. L'acteur seul sait qu'il en est d'autres, et non des moindres, au guichet, chaque soir.

16. On n'imagine pas le nombre d'acteurs qui vivent et travaillent pour le spectacle.

17. Je parle au hasard et il tombe sur moi.

18. Que voit un acteur chez un autre acteur ? il voit ce qu'il n'a pas misé et qui a été joué et perdu par celui-là.

19. On dirait l'aube d'un monde nouveau : les acteurs se mettent à nous ressembler.

20. Il prend nettement le pli : à quoi ressemblait-il déjà avant le repas-sage ?

21. Donnant dans l'onanisme, il perd le sens des affaires, donnant-donnant.

22. Je veux dire la vie côte à côte des hasards et des mots.

23. Une image est accusée d'avoir montré une chose cachée, elle est dans toutes les têtes, et le monde entier s'est retrouvé de son côté : juste une image et le monde s'y retrouve.

24. Lors d'une terrifiante première migraine, il posa clairement le problème de sa vie : il est né hobereau prussien, il meurt montagnard italien, et il fit table rase de de son pays et d'une nappe.

25. Peut être : ce qui l'est le peut déjà.

26. Laisser faire chacun dans son domaine et se boucher le nez en entrant.

27. L'acteur s'enrôle et déserte une vie.

28. Avoir peur de l'acteur, c'est rêver l'homme derrière la chaleur du masque.

29. Je n'ai rien de l'homme, c'est mon alibi.

30. Au désordre d'un vers sans pieds, il préfère celui des doigts d'une main.

31. Depuis le premier, tous les livres que j'ai lus ne parlent que de moi; cela en est à un point que je me demande ce qu'il en est de ceux que je n'ai pas lus; dois-je m'inquiéter de ce qu'ils racontent à mon sujet ? et si ces livres ne racontent rien, comment puis-je les lire, moi, qui suis tout ?

32. Croire en une vérité et boire la lie de sa réalité.

33. Rencontrerait-on dieu, qu'on lui prendrait ses empreintes divinitales.

34. Obscurcir lentement sa pensée afin d'en accommoder la portée et être grand devant le monde.

35. Dès le début, sans lancer le dé, atteindre le but, et être sur sa faim.

36. Enfant, il est né sans que personne ne s'en rende compte. La mère, interrogée, parle d'un oubli cette nuit-là. Le père, mort, ne se remémorait pas un quelconque oubli. C'est le vent qui passait par là.

37. J'ai même vu des acteurs retenir leur souffle, parce qu'ils vivaient parmi les hommes, pour ne pas jouer.

38. Il distribua les acteurs sans les mélanger avant le spectacle.

39. Je pris ma chute pour un envol et faisant le point, je conclue à un dispersement total et proche de mes activités.

40. Sur le désir des hommes: on dira que les nuages et les chapeaux sont là pour cacher les dessins cochons croqués sur les crânes des hommes.

41. Cette vieille question, je lui ai déjà trouvé une réponse, il y a un instant.

42. Enfant, il parle et écrit au hasard : il a des choses à lui dire.

43. Dieu est khâkhâ, croyez-en ma lourde expérience.

44. Chercher droit devant un détour connu et se trouver devant la troisième porte à droite dans le couloir.

45. Je porte haut en moi l'idée que l'homme est bas et je vois clair en moi sa cime et son abîme, l'ensemble, au rez-de-chaussée.

46. En 1987, le monde pleurait de toutes ses armes.

47. Par hasard il entend ce qui le sauve.

48. Le monde, qui est rond, tourne carrément mal : cherchez et aplanissez les angles.

49. Au commencement dire la table et ne pas savoir qu'elle est d'écoute.

50. Ce jour-là, je décidai d'en rester là : des mots vivront la suite.

51. Jésus n'est pas mort en croix, il est mort hanté.

52. Sur la route, regarder toujours derrière soi et se peigner devant la glace avant de partir.

53. Comment fait-il pour cacher le long couloir que ses yeux laissent éclairés la nuit?

54. La mer retire ses cartes le long des plages ocres : on dira que je suis le premier grain de sable touché par de vagues connaissances.

55. Se défaire de tout ce qui a été fait sans toucher aux nœuds.

56. Le réel m'enchante comme toutes les histoires courtes.

57. La vérité est l'unique mensonge qui court sous les jupes de la réalité.

58. En 1987, un homme, une fausse barbe, un nom de poupée, irritèrent un pays à l'endroit qui le démangeait et un Procès fut fait pour raser de près qui fit perdre des plumes aux dames de France.

59. Bien vu, bien dit et déjà si jeune.

60. La vérité se doit à elle-même de n'en rien faire : sinon qu'en dirait-on ?

61. Mes yeux vont mieux bien qu'il ne soit pas encore question de les sortir ensemble sur les sentiers de ma montagne.

62. Connaître le fond, pousser des talons, et voler au-dessus des montagnes.

63. Savoir brutalement ce que savoir veut dire et le faire taire.

64. J'emporte ce nuage pour qu'il pleuve les misères du monde.

65. Enfant, c'est déjà un homme qui vit seul par la force des choses. Il ne regarde pas sur les dépenses altruistes, ni sur les bénéfices. Il passe à la caisse les fins de semaine. Il connaît les calculs des hommes mesquins.

66. Entre chien cet loup, l'image tremble et la retransmission s'interrompt : ne sachant pas à quoi elle a affaire, l'image préfère se troubler puis jurer.

67. Hors le hasard, pas de nécessité dans le monde.

68. La mémoire qui sert aux acteurs se trouve usée quand elle parvient jusqu'aux hommes qui ne vivent alors que des premiers actes.

69. Un acteur joue son rôle et le perd en fin de partie.

70. Le chef, face à l'orchestre et la musique, évolue comme l'acteur, il ne sait pas en jouer et la musique passe par-delà ses épaules.

71. Les portes noires ferment les âmes nobles des enfants : les clés d'or sont dans les commodes des pères, des mères ; les oiseaux tapent du bec contre le marbre des marches des maisons familiales ; on dira qu'on joue et que je suis un enfant ; maintenant, la porte se ferme et les papas et les mamans retiennent leurs souffles ; le marbre est sec, la maison froide, je décide de commencer une vie en oiseau.

72. Pensant l'être et ne l'étant pas, l'acteur gagne sur chaque tableau ayant appris les deux rôles.

73. Juste une parole pour avancer un pas jusqu'à l'improbable sens d'un mélange de bruits, de sons et de musiques : la vie est un opéra.

74. Si le jouisseur fait de vice vertu et l'ascète de hasard nécessité, alors je suis vertueux par hasard et nécessiteux par vice.

75. Voyant venir de loin, j'ai eu le temps de faire le tour de moi-même.

76. Si la vérité est femme, alors l'homme a tort, donc la femme est mensonge car je suis homme. Mais si la vérité est homme, c'est que la femme a tort, or je suis homme et j'ai toujours raison.

77. On sait des choses sur un acteur alors qu'il ne sait rien sur nous.

78. A-t-on jamais vraiment pensé à l'impossible réussite des sociétés humaines qui survivent hors des régions les plus limpides de l'air ?

79. Il est de notoriété publique que rien.

80. Savoir de quoi on parle et qui est on.

81. Il faut dire que pour, l'homme réel toute vérité est bonne à dire pourvu qu'elle s'accroche ferme aux wagons du train d'histoires dites depuis l'enfance.

82. On dira que tu arrêtes ta philosophie pour aujourd'hui, tu mets tes godillots, tu marches dans une ville allemande, tu te payes une putain, et quand tu reviens, ta philosophie en a terminé, seule.

83. Une profession est une épine dans le dos de la vie.

84. M'aimant frappant, je l'aimais frappée ; s'aimant frappé, il l'aimait frappante ; sa Carmen adorée.

85. On donne aux acteurs le crédit : de leurs rôles en débitant sur le compte de leurs années.

86. On ne dira pas que l'acteur agit contre son gré, on reconnaîtra qu'il fait quelque chose pour la communauté des hommes.

87. Il avait des désirs de mort pour le chant des opéras qui étaient des envies d'airs et de mots.

88. Chaque soir, à la même heure, en un même lieu, un acteur se loge une balle dans la tête.

89. Est-ce donc une science que de saisir l'âme humaine dans toute son étendue, ou alors on réfuterait l'âme dans l'homme ? pourrait-on dénier l'existence de l'âme, à voir l'homme mettre ses deux mains sur le sexe à l'appel du prêtre ?

90. Dans les théâtres, la nuit, les hommes craignent les gestes lourds de sens des acteurs en scène.

91. On espère l'évènement d'une vie et on est ce père, qui sait, que ça passera par là.

92. Faire l'acteur et prendre pour soi l'addition, même lorsque le conte n'est pas apprivoisé.

93. D'où vient qu'une exécution est plus navrante qu'un meurtre, sinon à cause de l'absence de représailles ?

94. Des femmes, l'homme seul ne sait qu'une chose : ce qu'on en dit.

95. Pour être ce qu'on aurait dû, payons déjà de ce qu'on est.

96. Carmen : la carte impitoyable a répété la mort jusqu'à ce qu'elle s'ensuive, la main dans la main, sur le chemin qui mène au port.

97. On l'a toujours su et pourtant, toute la vie, il ne s'agira que de ça.

98. Admirer dans l'homme ce qui signifie que le haut est fragile alors que le bas blesse.

99. Je lance le dé sur le théâtre des opérations et je récolte les injures des comédiens armés.

100. Très tôt, j'ai su me dégager de l'obligation de savoir s'en dégager, juste pour faire comme on m'a dit.

101. Ce que les acteurs et les actrices font ensemble ne regarde pas le théâtre.

102. On n'a pas idée et on veut le monde à ses pieds.

103. Sur la brèche : le cri des enfants fait pencher la balance là où ça fait mal.

104. Penser ce qu'on veut du divin et y rester allongé toute une nuit.

105. J'ai trop bien saisi son désir profond pour préférer me laisser porter par les petites vagues de sa surface.

106. Dieu connaît la musique et il a oublié de la mettre sur les paraboles de son fils.

107. Que celui qui n'a jamais fauté me lance sa première phrase écrite au visage.

108. On voit la connerie des semblables lorsqu'on entend le rire des différents.

109. On ne doit pas sous-estimer la force du réel lors des séances de détection de mensonges que sont les confessions religieuses.

110. Chaque fois que dans le monde un acteur joue un enfant meurt.

111. Casser du sucre sur son propre dos et avoir juste une pensée salée pour les histoires de famille.

112. Il en est de l'innocence des enfants comme de la nécessité du hasard : une question de dés pipés quelque soit le nombre jusqu'auquel on sait leur conter des histoires une fois la face gagnante visible sur le drap de lit.

113. Prendre le chemin de la cuisine, croiser la mère, et ne pas oublier combien il a fallu de temps de cuisson et de poivre.

114. Une phrase écrite avec de vrais mots peut-elle mentir ?

115. A la réflexion, les vues d'un pays sur un autre pays ne dépendent que de l'angle décrit par la fenêtre et le miroir placés de part et d'autre de la frontière : on ne mentionnera pas que les douaniers sont triés sur le volet et qu'ils ne passent jamais de l'autre côté du miroir.

116. Se proposer pour défendre la cause et mourir à cause d'elle.

117. Rester là, solitaire et glacé, devant la porte ouverte du réfrigérateur.

118. Si dieu avait écouté Carmen, il en aurait fait tout un plat de petits noms de dieu.

119. Connaît-on réellement tout ce que peut l'homme quand on ne sait rien de sa famille?

120. Un acteur ne croit jamais ce qu'on lui dit car il réplique sans cesse.

121. Allongé au coin d'un pré, j'ai vu l'horreur d'une vache immaculée de sa propre merde.

122. Quand il ne joue pas, l'acteur laisse croire à un trou de mémoire.

123. Prendre un mot au pied de la lettre et le relever jusqu'à la phrase.

124. Pourrir une relation et être assis dessus lorsqu'on la coupe.

125. Prendre une jambe à son cou et laisser l'autre à l'étrier.

126 Je pensai défaire une fois pour toutes certains liens
     qui m'attachent à la mort : mais je me trompai dans
     les fils et perdis mon parachute.

127. Faire croître une image et, de fait, ne plus y croire.

128. —Tu deviens ce que tu es. —Comment le sais-tu ?
     —Je l'étais avant toi. —Qu'es-tu devenu ? —Ce que
     tu seras.

129. Il est beaucoup attendu d'un acteur en fin de course :
     sa dernière peau, nos propres pas dans sa foulée et
     quand il franchit la ligne, l'espoir d'endosser son
     costume de mort.

130. Lorsque personne ne les regarde, les images se
     regardent-elles?

131. Certaines personnes vont jusqu'à payer pour voir
     jouer des acteurs.

132. De l'homme, l'homme ne sait qu'une chose : ce qu'il
     se raconte.

133. On se trompera rarement si l'on ramène les actions
     vertueuses à la diarrhée, les criminelles à l'éthylisme
     et son chien à ma voisine.

134. Connaître bien une chose qu'on apprécie et, ne cachant rien à papa, avouer que c'est maman.

135. Paul imposa Pierre à ses amis et y mit du sien.

136. L'homme a tout imaginé : un dieu, une morale, un plaisir et il n'a aimé en tout que deux choses : tuer et mettre au monde.

137. J'ai aimé sans aimer être sans y être avec vous mais sans eux.

138. Le monde s'échappe autour de nous, car à l'intérieur nous en savons assez sur lui pour l'enfermer.

139. Il ne s'habitue à rien, il vit, c'est tout.

140. Permuter circulairement la guerre et la paix et ne plus savoir par laquelle on a commencé.

141. Dieu porte la poisse en son être comme le simple porte dieu entre ses feuilles.

142. Celui-ci tente franchement sa chance et la convaincant perd tout espoir de la séduire.

143. Je connais la fin du morceau mais suis tombé sur la tête et ne sais plus de quoi parle au début de la musique.

144. Tordre le cou des faussaires, tailler dans le flots des pitiés et gagner en force la partie.

145. Comprendre ce qui fait tenir : il s'agit des quelques coups qu'on peut mettre entre soi et le monde, je parle de ceux-là.

146. Cet acteur a joué tous les rôles et il ne manque qu'un titre à son répertoire : moi, acteur.

147. Tout dire d'un enfant et le faire avouer.

148. Un aveugle ne connaît des choses que ce qu'on lui en dit ; nous, qui avons tout appris des choses, serions-nous sourds? ou muets ? ou quoi.

149. Il a dépensé l'or de sa vie à spéculer sur le cours des fleuves de son petit territoire : savait-il bien de quel côté s'épanchait la source ?

150. Je n'ai aucune idée de ce qu'elle est donc je n'y pense pas.

151. L'acteur fait peu souvent le tour du théâtre trop occupé qu'il est à en habiter le centre.

152. Les acteurs ne sont jamais dedans, ils sont devant : c'est un véritable drame pour l'acteur que jouer de face quand il ne s'agit que de cacher son cul.

153. On se l'est toujours demandé pour autant que l'on s'en souvienne; on ne se souvient jamais de quoi.

154. Alors que les hommes défilent, il interroge chaque visage : quelle est la réponse ?

155. Percevant le miroir derrière lui, il laissait les dossiers s'entretenir puis se clore.

156. S'entendre dire qu'on va le dire et le dire en y allant.

157. A la lecture d'une pièce de théâtre, l'acteur fait le tour du propriétaire : on n'a jamais vu la couleur d'un rideau ou le motif d'une tapisserie influer sur le choix d'un rôle.

158. D'un geste, il fit un roman de ses pensées et d'un mot, il fabriqua une philosophie de ses histoires.

159. Comme on fait son lit, on se couche.

160. Mieux vaut vivre dans le faux que suivre très tôt l'homme à la faux.

161. En initialisant sa vie, il fit que l'écran effaçât jusqu'à la première lettre de son patronyme : tout est à faire et le programme sans fin.

162. Sait-on bien voir dans la nature quelque chose qui n'a rien à voir avec l'homme ?

163. Cette rue parle à travers cette fenêtre et ne se doute pas des oreilles de cette chambre à côté, et ce ne sont pas les murs qui écoutent.

164. Les maux de tête s'écrivent et ne se ressemblent pas.

165. Se défaire lentement d'un préjugé et être sur la liste d'attente du prochain.

166. Les secrets replis de l'âme humaine ne résistent pas aux repassages successifs des coups de pieds ferrés au cul de la vie.

167. Dessiner la vie d'un enfant et gommer les coups incertains.

168. Connaîtrait-on la mort, qu'on n'en voudrait rien savoir.

169. Voit-on réellement les hommes s'aimer les uns les autres quand l'hiver n'en gèle que la moitié ?

170. L'espérance est ce qui est caché au fond du coffre quand toutes les saloperies se sont envolées par la porte blindée.

171. Je commence d'ores et déjà à comprendre la raison de tout cela, une sorte d'effet spécial à long terme.

172. Ils ne savent pas ce qu'ils font, et n'en faisant rien, ils n'en sauraient pas plus.

173. Il a dit, voyageant autour de sa chambre, ouvrant portes et fenêtres, à la cantonade, que, ces jours derniers, la montagne et la mer lui ont parlé italien.

174. Tu prends les enfants, on ne sait pas, ils sont parfois les plus grands.

175. Dire du mal d'un acteur et, ce faisant, lui voler son meilleur rôle.

176. Succéder pacifiquement à un bonheur tranquille et entendre les trompettes sans succès.

177. Pourfendre de tout cœur le chrétien et se fendre pour le cœur d'une chrétienne.

178. La mort, je n'en sais rien, je n'en connais rien, j'en entends parler, encore, une fois de plus.

179. On n'a jamais dit que dieu était bon sinon qu'il avait eu le bon goût de ne pas se laisser goûter une fois pour toutes.

180. En 2007, de vieilles et vilaines choses furent dites, on les crut et certaines amitiés brunes et odorantes furent perdues, alors on se rassembla autour de son seul nom, France.

181. La pensée indigeste qui occupe mon esprit a longtemps voyagé le long de mon intestin.

182. On est rien comme on naît tout, me dit une mère vidée.

183. Tu regardes par la fenêtre de la chambre et cela se passe aux fourneaux.

184. Etre au centre de la cuisine, lire la recette à haute et intelligible voix et briser l'idéal chrétien.

185. Respecter une minute le silence.

186. On ne peut rien pour une idée qui ne sait pas nager, on peut seulement la noyer dans le chagrin de ses détracteurs.

187. A quoi s'attendre de sa part sinon qu'elle est plus grosse que celle des autres ?

188. Il éduque l'enfant comme il conduit la voiture dont les rétroviseurs sont tournés vers ce qui advient.

189. Un enfant a dit à un homme qu'il était petit.

190. Dieu est bon comme une fille.

191. Dominer le vrai monde et se pendre parmi les étoiles rougeoyantes du communisme.

192. Un mot est mort, faute d'orthographe.

193. Laisser dire les autres comme ils sentent et se boucher le nez.

194. En détournant le regard de son abîme, j'ai rencontré le mien.

195. Découvrir peu à peu la raison qui fait naître : il s'agit de ces choses que mangent les hommes et les femmes, je parle des coups.

196. Bien être ce qu'on est bien.

197. Les derniers acteurs seront les premiers hommes ou ne seront rien.

198. Dieu met le doigt sur le nœud pendant que l'homme use ses semelles à marcher dans le désert : ce dernier ne voit pas la taille des lacets qui le tiennent.

199. Aimer le prochain sans savoir conjuguer au futur « conjuguer au présent ».

200. Les acteurs croient toujours en ce qu'ils font, tout ce mensonge.

201. Ressentir la fulgurance d'une percée possible et être comme un con à l'entrée de l'orifice.

202. Corroborons à l'action des hommes, jusque dans la collaboration.

203. Une image persiste et imagine qu'elle est un signe.

204. Dieu aime les enfants de Marie et il en profite.

205. Tu regardes le vrai fond de la grotte, tu vois les vraies choses s'agiter, tu comprends la vraie raison de tout et tout, tu sors de chez toi sans ta clé.

206. Je suis, quand j'y pense, à l'origine de ces mots, comme le fleuve est, quand il y pense, à l'origine de sa source.

207. Sur la table, les alignements successifs ordonnent le monde autour de l'assiette et permettent aux grains de riz de ne pas coller malgré les larmes des dieux détrônés.

208. Dieu et tous ses saints ont été ce qui s'est fait de mieux en matière de soutien.

209. En 2002, on espérait beaucoup de 2007.

210. L'acteur détient par-devers lui le secret d'une humanité maîtresse du masque.

211. Regarder à l'intérieur de la maison et recevoir au visage la teneur en terroir chaud et gras de son ventre.

212. Renoncer à la joie d'être, s'annoncer en maître.

213. Les mémoires d'un acteur ne sont pas du passé sinon d'un présent toujours répété et sous les feux de la rampe.

214. Il y a peu, il connut une autre version de l'histoire : venaient après l'habituel, un frère, une sœur, son ange, un cousin, une cousine, des oncles, des tantes, parfois un encore jeune et toujours une bête, un autre genre.

215. L'acteur perd le sens des réalités en gagnant sur l'essence de l'homme.

216. Savoir sans avoir à demander et oublier : la femme retient, l'homme détient, l'enfant s'y tient.

217. Tu prends le lit conjugal, tu vois les oreillers, on ne s'y entend pas mais on écoute ; tu regardes les deux dedans, tu comptes pour eux et tu le vois ; tu ne comprends pas, tu écoutes, avec les oreillers, tu sais déjà, bon.

218. S'emporter loin, très loin, et lâcher la poignée, un soir, l'été.

219. Verser dans l'anomalie, déboucher sur une maladie.

220. On imagine le rêve de l'autre quand à l'image il ferme les yeux.

221. Regarder chez l'homme ce qui peut se détacher selon les pointillés de sa lâcheté.

222. Permettre au monde d'exister autour de soi et se voir encadré avec la fenêtre pleine de ciel ouverte au fond du tableau.

223. Dire ce qu'on dit et mentir; ne pas dire ce qu'on dit et ne pas mentir ; dire une chose, ne pas mentir et le dire ; dire autre chose, ne pas mentir et ne pas le dire ; sans mentir, ne pas dire ce qu'on dit ; sans mentir, dire ce qu'on ne dit pas ; sans mentir, dire qu'on ment et mentir sans mentir.

224. Tomber sans vie et se relever mort tout de bon ; avoir vu l'au-delà et s'y être oublié ou ennuyé, selon ses opinions politiques.

225. Je m'oublie salement chaque jour que dieu fait.

226. Les acteurs s'entendent entre eux pour ne pas être sourds aux bruits des hommes.

227. Que dira-t-on aux enfants de l'amour, lorsque naturellement ils tendront leurs culs à la concupiscence des autres enfants de l'amour ?

228. Il donne de la confiture aux cochons comme de bonnes intentions aux prêtres gourmands.

229. J'ai beaucoup aimé être avec vous, même si je n'en ai rien eu à faire.

230. Se demander pourquoi et ne plus savoir quand c'était.

231. Y aller pour tendre l'oreille et se la faire tirer.

232. Hasardons nos pensées sur le terrain des leurres.

233. J'ai bien aimé vous regarder faire, même si j'ai fait que vous me regardiez, vous.

234. Le hasard fait mal aux choses.

235. Soit dit en passant et ainsi soit-il : *amor fati*.

236. Briser l'enveloppe des choses et perdre l'adresse par retour du courrier.

237. Les voix de l'acteur sont interprétables.

238. On préférera aux ardeurs de l'actrice les vices de l'acteur.

239. Ne lui dites rien qu'il ne sache déjà, il est persuadé du contraire.

240. Ceci dit, je mens.

241. Il se torture l'esprit pour échapper au divin alors que ce dernier est en cuir noir et qu'il a déjà réglé la consultation.

242. Les désordres de nos acteurs font sourire les ordres de nos troupes en armes.

243. Affamer son besoin d'âmes mal famées.

244. Prendre une femme et perdre les restes.

245. On dira que chercher le contact des corps encore est plus recherché que d'avoir le tact de ne pas dire ce qu'on désire à tort.

246. Sous le nom de chaque acteur ne se cache pas toujours celui des parents de ce dernier

247. La cruauté envers les animaux chez les enfants et les Italiens est quelque chose de compréhensible : ou alors c'est ne rien comprendre à l'innocence de ces derniers.

248. J'ai vu ce jour des maisons italiennes, hautes et rouges ; ce que j'en dis ne vaut que par ce que j'en ai vu ; parfois quelque chose était écrit que je n'ai pas lu.

249. On te dit que tout se fait tôt ou tard, un jour ou l'autre, et tu penses à l'horloge qui déploie les heures et les dates en chapelet autour de ton cou, nœud après nœud.

250. Je me suis donné pour tâche d'isoler du concept ce qui peut être roman.

251. Dites des mensonges et soyez dans le vrai, la réalité veille.

252. Son apparence est trompeuse car il tient en partie de l'éléphant.

253. Donner dans l'incomparable et perdre au change, comparaison faite.

254. Pour accéder aux enfances vraies des petits, il enregistre les papas et les mamans.

255. On a vu des hommes se taper la tête contre les murs du son parce qu'ils étaient sourds.

256. En 1987, les sexes des femmes, ouverts et parfois pénétrés par les sexes des hommes, défrayèrent les chroniques des gouvernants droitiers et de France.

257. Disons qu'en gros les hommes sont petits et que, petit à petit, les femmes sont grandes : l'un ira-t-il sans l'autre ? prophétise le tailleur.

258. Tu prends l'ordre immuable des choses du monde viable, tu serres, tu serres, c'est sale dans la paume.

259. Etre d'attaque au saut du lit et perdre la guerre en posant le mauvais pied : un début de journée qui finit mal.

260. Les acteurs n'en sont pas moins des hommes : les femmes sont plus que ça.

261. Tout dire, tout décrire, tout expliquer à l'acteur et voir ce que cela donne sur la scène du théâtre.

262. Lors de son dernier voyage au loin, il prit connaissance de sa maison natale et, essayant une clé après l'autre, se trouve enfermé à l'extérieur; un homme passa par là qui, s'il avait été son père, lui aurait ouvert ; lorsqu'une femme lui dit qu'il devait rentrer chez lui, il sut bien qu'il n'avait pas de mère ; la prochaine fois, il téléphonerait avant de rentrer.

263. Sophiste, j'écris que je le suis ; sage, je pense l'être ; philosophe, vous l'êtes qui lisez que je le suis.

264. D'où tient-on que la vie ait un sens ? On le tient de derrière les fagots.

265. Croire avec un grand C et y avoir cru avec un grand U, le lui avoir dit à elle avec un grand L et ne pas faire le geste.

266. Il invente ses propres remèdes et par des bains intérieurs se purifie de toute la matière indigeste que la vie lui a fait avaler.

267. On dit que la mort prend sur elle tous les torts faits aux hommes : ils n'en pensent pas moins à propos de la vie et de toute la saloperie.

268. Perdre un peu de ce qu'on est en gagnant une dernière fois un peu de la magnificence du ciel sans dieu.

269. Dans l'angle d'un pré, j'ai vu l'horreur d'une vache qui chassait sans arrêts les mouches, de la queue, des oreilles.

270. Les yeux ronds voient tout au fond, la tête carrée tape au tréfonds, il a posé sa tête sur les corps des femmes, il a tapé ses yeux aux murs des âmes, on dirait une philosophie quand même, une légère philosophie qu'on amène.

271. Tu prends la déroute de quarante, les français marchaient sur la route, quand même.

272. Au dernier jour, il étonnera le monde en parlant de sa vache, son chien et ses filles, et ce sera son fils qui s'assoira sur le couvercle de son tombeau, pour continuer à se taire.

273. On désespère vraiment quoiqu'on en dise à partir du jour où on espère quoiqu'on fasse en un petit désespoir de convenance.

274. Qu'est-ce qu'une suite de hasards sinon l'immense chance d'avoir eu le bonheur de connaître cela ?

275. Un homme prend un parapluie et s'en donne un coup sur la tête : voilà une façon contre la dépression, un coup contre la pluie, à la place d'un père malléable et sous la misère du monde.

276. Espérer, c'est désespérer à rebours.

277. On ne sait jamais et pourtant il n'y a rien dont on ne parle pas.

278. Faire l'enfant et brûler le croquis.

279. Effacer la dernière image puis compter sur la prochaine pour se souvenir de celle d'avant et ainsi de suite.

280. Au détour d'une phrase imprimée, un mot s'exila et réfuta tout le livre.

281. On a trop vu et trop bien compris ce genre d'histoire : un père, une mère, un enfant, une maison et parfois un trop vieux, une trop vieille, ce genre-là.

282. C'est un acteur, il ne sait pas jouer la comédie.

283. Voir de loin et perdre le détail de l'accouplement des êtres et des chaînes, nus.

284. Dieu aime tout ce que je fais et où que je le fasse.

285. Au commencement, dire OUI et apprendre son nom.

286. Pour comprendre sa destinée, laisser faire le destin et s'asseoir sur les talons.

287. Je sais que je ne sais rien mais je vois bien que tout est là.

288. Se surprendre à dire, quand on pisse, qu'on ne voit pas son petit zizi et être seul.

289. Fou qu'il était, il vécut voici cent ans ; lorsqu'il vivait, il pensait souvent mourir ; il est mort en 1900, à la fin de sa vie ; il ne vit rien, fou qu'il était.

290. Quand il entrait à l'école de la vie, il s'en sortait la mort dans l'âme.

291. Pleurer une déconvenue alors qu'elles viennent de partir.

292. Enoncer le lieu du rendez-vous et perdre jusqu'à l'idée de quand c'était, le prix compris.

293. Enfant, le jour où il connut toute l'histoire, décida de ne plus jamais grandir ; les nombreux gestes qu'Enfant entreprit et répéta lui permirent de tenir la distance ; avançant pas à pas, jour après jour, il ne grandit pas d'un seul centimètre ; la nature de son mal fit qu'Enfant resta ce qu'il est depuis l'année dernière, un enfant.

294. Lire la vie du philosophe et vivre à la lettre une pensée qui vit ; lire les écrits du philosophe et écrire une vie qui pense.

295. Tout acteur aura un jour dans sa vie l'occasion d'être sauvé par son costume et son chapeau : encore faudra-t-il qu'il les prenne à sa taille pour ne pas sauver un autre que lui-même.

296. L'acteur est un centaure, à moitié vrai, à moitié faux, et avec des ailes d'ange à la tête.

297. Cet acteur découvre le grand large et ses émotions en cabotinant le long des côtes spectatrices.

298. A l'avenir, les vrais hommes seront les hommes réels, et la vérité, qui est femme, sera triste.

299. Dire la vérité et s'en remettre.

300. Vivre contre quand la vie est pour et réciproquement, dieu merci.

301. Je me couche, c'est fini, rideau.

Dear Alain,

I propose the following remarks to you, as a letter to write, as a conversation to invent, as a bird who reflects the sky of frosts and the buried suns, in the form of some untimely questions. To return or to refuse, to give or to take, as you intend in the language that is yours, that same exigency that carries your astonishing à corps défendant.

Nathanaël

My Body's Returns, by Nathanaël

Alain Jugnon

1. *How did the theatre arrive at you?*

The theatre arrived at me frontally, like a train on a departures platform. I could not, being an adolescent, not want to speak where I wasn't speaking and not want to be there since I had never been: first, I did theatre to make love to people I was afraid of. A question of power and of the body's work already. Until the age of 18, since I didn't read and I didn't like anything, I was lacking in everything affectively. I invented my first love, there, it had to be staged and there would be a woman who would come forward to speak to me. Writing was another story: first the stage and the woman, then I worked. I read fairly quickly Adamov, Beckett and Genet. It's a bit of a lie because I don't really remember the first play I read. I remember in high school having performed with other young people some Sartre and some Ionesco, only to leave them and find myself mad and alone reading all of Beckett, that's it: I read Beckett, and on the stage I wanted to see before me Vladimir and Estragon, Mercier and Camier, Molloy and Malone. And no more woman, the theatre was that disappearance for me. How I became a writer by losing sight of the woman on stage. Because in the '80's in Lyon I worked in a beautiful theatre, Les Ateliers, with Gilles Chavassieux: the theatre arrived at me with Gilles since I still love him like the father I invented for myself on stage.

2. *Tristesse and Trieste. Nietzsche as a way of autofiguring? (The city as autorretrato, the name as before, the body to belie, or not).*

Yes, I am Barcelona and Bel Ami, I am Nietzsche and Nanaki (certainly one of Antonin Artaud's childhood names) and I am also Lyon and Louise Brooks (as Lulu, and as my daughter Louise), and it is yet again the stage set forth to write what the woman is telling me, not the other one, not them, the woman that I am not, her name in *Calcutta désert*. The *corps défendant* is a body on stage and body in life-joy, or life-tragedy, or life-death. It is still a stage that fascinates-fabricates-ferrets me,

80

following the founding experience, dreamed and detested, of my first vision of David Lynch's film, a very long time ago: *Eraserhead*. The songstress behind the radiator definitively sent me there, it is my yesterday eternally, I am behind the radiator but in front of the stage, they are all there, in front. I am in number, the *innammerated* of all the names and all the cities of a life. There and names and cities, that's all.

3.   *Suffering, jubilation (sensitivities).*

I ask myself the question of evil without speaking it so as not to wake the children. Good is the only absolute that fits the body for a human, so Hannah Arendt wrote, I am before this woman also: the philosopher that I love; and it isn't a matter of ideas or of books, it's another scene I am making for myself, it's sensible in the sense that I love that she exists and works in philosophy and because I am a name and a life before the name and the life of this very woman, that I love. In keeping with the order of an absolute necessity: the joy – against death – of thinking, of becoming what one is, like on a plate of fruit, many oranges, a collective enunciation of/for all (the animals and the prisoners just as Deleuze has it): at home, to defend myself in body, there is my Nietzsche in Turin and my Genet in Chatila.

4. *Poetry – theatre – philosophy. What relayed itineraries? Their approach.*

In fact, at home, poetry, theatre, and philosophy, are precisely one and the same: it is the history of my reading of books, that trinity which makes me a writer-reader and the reverse. A life is the immanence of a reader of worlds, of a writer of places and names. Nothing else to write today: in this order which goes from theatre to poetry. Right now I am the poetry of what I want to read: this morning it was *Les jours et les nuits* by Alfred Jarry. I had this morning the chance of never having read it, I began to read it this morning, I am henceforth entirely Jarry-Joy to write tomorrow my book on Gilles Deleuze. To become in this arrangement what I have been living every day for thirty years, it has to be most closely to Antonin Artaud, more and more as an old madman or as a big wolf, because he assembled the plans for a poetry-theatre-philosophy life: there is him and Bataille and Genet and Jarry and there was Nietzsche the father and the friend of philosopher-artists. I like this house of bodies together.

5. *The crossing of the Atlantides. The body and its defenses.*

Bodies, a life, the book. Fuck the capital letter. It's body-life-book. *Livre, c'est libre.* I am the lower case to pass from north-to-south and from east-to-west, always through the central ocean: the atlanteans and the caryatids can't take me anymore, the post is relayed to my oar. I am the African and the mariner, heart set upon the body. When I undertake my voyage, I lie down in italics. In *Le voyage au bout de la nuit*, what is most strong and heaviest, is that Céline's Africa is a New York multiplied by thousands of humanities and by all the bodies defending themselves alone and beautiful. I love Céline for the bodies and his defense. In spite of them. Literature is all that remains.

Smallpox for the Millenary

Nathanaël

La guerre ne l'avait pas rendu intact à la vie.

LÉON WERTH

During the War to end War, some time between the Baskervilles and Agent Orange, there was the small matter of a typhoid outbreak among field soldiers that the French war ministry sought to control through the enforcement of a vaccine. The risks of the epidemic were matched by the risks to which soldiers were exposed by this experimental inoculation, and so with the gangrenous trenches, and the steady threat of ballistics, the internal matter of the body's hygiene was a further front on which to defend oneself. None of which was received without some form of resistance, and nor could any claim immunity. So the soldiers defended their bodies, just as they defended against their bodies, and as is the case in and outside of great works of literature, with varying degrees of reprisal, punitive measures, and success, leading, at times to the great catch-all: death. The edicts and decrees of course assume the form of national dictates, subsuming the one into the many, and abrogating, thereby, the necessity for, or the right to, autonomy. It is no secret that battlefields are the experimental grounds of chemical catastrophe, biological assault, and what are often referred to as medical advancements. Mustard gas and blood transfusions provide two apparently tidy examples. Never mind that the swamps doused with Napalm still carry their burn, or that the birds stifled their song at Birkenau. Nor that, generally speaking, war itself is a great ground of merciless trials carried out against populations, civilian or otherwise. "As you are about to leave, you say that you aren't vaccinated against typhoid and you burn your record and you say: 'When I was asked whether I was vaccinated, I thought that it was for smallpox.' You're given eight days in the slammer, but you've got a month to go." (Léon Werth). For the soldier cuckolded by the state, it is a kind of sentencing, and in either case, whatever the military's position, "the army" as Kaji scances in Kobayashi Masaki's *Ningen no jōken* (The Human Condition), "is the enemy".

a body, in spite may have nothing to do with any of the above. But between eight days and a month, there is enormous room for error. And the question might arise as to which side of the bars will constitute the proving ground. Even admitting that the bars have symbolic value, and that *nothing to do* is precisely where one is mobilized. As Jugnon's text declaims: "It is of public notoriety that nothing." Provided, of course, that one is able to know "who is one."

à corps défendant names the exact tension between a body in action and a body's inaction. And translation is here most magnanimously of no help in elucidating the torqued idiomatic expression that has expunged the reflexivity of *à son corps défendant*, for which English offers as a literal equivalent *the resistance to an attack* while expressing idiomatic *regret*. The coexistence of these two contrary efforts in this locution prepare the ground for a battlefield of philosophical ailment and semantic reprisal the gauge for which abandons the usual referents. The result, for the anglophone reader, is a rageful distance from an identifiable torment. Just as the war is subsumed into its obliquity, the language of the war is full of faces "visible on the bedsheet." But isn't history, too, a concatenation of street names and dwellings, more or less flung open to public view, and swept into "the wind passing through." Lineage is a form of melancholy made of finished philosophies.

For José Ortega y Gasset, "even before entering the fray, [man] already carries a wound in his temple." He means time. And if the time of translation abounds in this kind of belatedness, it is made more pressing by the kind of present that is at stake in *a body, in spite*. Jugnon takes the man with his wound and declares him to be alive: "It was always known and yet, all life long, it will only ever be a matter of that."

In his essay, *Athéologiques*, the author provides what may be this text's loophole: "The name poses its dead: the name shows contempt to the living by saying clearly and distinctly the infinite individuation, the theatre of permanent death, which is all life and which is all thought." It is a long march from France's inroads of 1940 to becoming "the son of one's own events" (Gilles Deleuze). The "philosopher-body," such as it is contended by Jugnon, is a porous fortification, and if the hole widens inward, it is because its greatest capacity is also its most visibly hidden.

Having now crossed the Atlantic into this English of the Americas, *a body, in spite* will have other smallpoxes to contend with. Against the ripest forms of violence in the guise of cultivated amnesia, and fascisms of the everyday, Jugnon's work reminds history of its regimens, and the present of its pettiest details. It is against the erasure of these details that Alain Jugnon places these words back in the entrails of the body, where the mouth is summoned to its defenses.

Works Cited

Léon Werth. *Clavel chez les majors,* 1918.

Alain Jugnon. *Athéologiques. L'humanisme, le communisme et Charles Péguy,* 2016.

Kobayashi Masaki. *Ningen no jōken,* 1959-1961. Tr. unspecified.

José Ortega y Gasset. "Miseria y esplendor de la traducción," 1937. Tr. E.G. Miller.

Epigraph: War had not returned him intact to life. (Werth)

Unattributed translations by Nathanaël

ALAIN JUGNON is a philosopher and writer. He has written for the theatre and has published essays and articles on Nietzsche, Artaud and Bataille. He is the editor of *Cahiers Artaud* (Éditions Les Cahiers) and the political and poetic journal *La contre attaque* (Éditions Pontcerq). Alain Jugnon's most recent books include *Contre Onfray* (Nouvelles Éditions Lignes); *Athéologiques, L'humanisme, le communisme et Charles Péguy* (Éditions Dasein) and *Artaud in Amerika* (Éditions Dernier Télégramme). *a body, in spite,* marks the first publication of a work by this important French thinker in English.

NATHANAËL is the author of more than a score of books written in English or in French, including *N'existe* (2017), *Feder* (2016), and *L'heure limicole* (2016). Translations include works by Édouard Glissant, Danielle Collobert, Hervé Guibert, Hilst Hilst and Catherine Mavrikakis.

NIGHTBOAT BOOKS

Nightboat Books, a nonprofit organization, seeks to develop audiences for writers whose work resists convention and transcends boundaries. We publish books rich with poignancy, intelligence, and risk. Please visit nightboat.org to learn more about us and how you can support our future publications.

The following individuals have supported the publication of this book. We thank them for their generosity and commitment to the mission of Nightboat Books:

Elizabeth Motika
Benjamin Taylor

In addition, this book has been made possible, in part, by a grant from the National Endowment for the Arts and the New York State Council on the Arts Literature Program.